Animal Disguises

KINGFISHER

LONDON & NEW YORK

Distributed in the U.S. by Macmillan, 175 Fifth Ave., New York, NY 10010

LIBRARY OF CONGRESS CATALOGING-IN-PUBLICATION DATA
Weber, Belinda.
Animal disguises/Belinda Weber.—1st ed.
p. cm.
1. Animal defenses—Juvenile literature. I. Title. II. Series.
QL759.W43 2004
591.47—dc22
2004000407

ISBN 978-0-7534-6162-4

Kingfisher books are available for special promotions and premiums. For details contact:
Special Markets Department, Macmillan, 175 Fifth Ave., New York, NY 10010.

For more information, please visit www.kingfisherbooks.com

First published in hardcover as *Kingfisher Young Knowledge: Animal Disguises* in 2004
First published in this format in 2007

Printed in China
2 4 6 8 10 9 7 5 3
2TR/0611/WKT/RNB(RNB)/140MA/F

Acknowledgments
The Publisher would like to thank the following for permission to reproduce their material. Every care has been taken
to trace copyright holders. However, if there have been unintentional omissions or failure to trace copyright holders,
we apologize and will, if informed, endeavor to make corrections in any future edition.
b = bottom, *c* = center, *l* = left, *t* = top, *r* = right

Cover Nature Picture Library (Naturepl); page 1 Ardea; 3 Naturepl; 4–5 Naturepl; 7 Naturepl; 8*b* Getty Images (Getty); 9*t* Oxford Scientific
Films (OSF); 10–11 Ardea; 11*t* Ardea; 11*b* Corbis; 12 Nature History Picture Agency (NHPA); 13*tr* Getty; 13*cl* OSF; 13*b* Corbis; 14*cl* OSF;
14*b* OSF; 15*tr* Fogden Photographs; 15*b* Naturepl; 16*tr* Ardea; 16*b* OSF; 17 Fogden Photographs; 18–19 Naturepl; 18*tl* Naturepl; 19*tr*
Fogden Photographs; 20–21 Corbis; 20*b* Ardea; 21*br* Ardea; 22–23 National Geographic Image Collection; 22*cl* NHPA; 23*tr* OSF; 24–25
National Geographic Image Collection; 24*bl* Ardea; 24*br* Ardea; 26*b* OSF; 27*t* Naturepl; 27*b* Naturepl; 28*cr* Fogden Photographs; 28*bl* OSF;
29*tr* OSF; 29*b* Corbis; 30*tl* Ardea; 30*b* Ardea; 31*t* Ardea; 31*br* Ardea; 32–33 Getty; 32*bl* Fainting Goat Association, U.S.; 33*tr* National
Geographic Image Collection; 34*t* Ardea; 34*b* Corbis; 35 Ardea; 36–37 Ardea; 36*bl* OSF; 37*tr* Naturepl; 38–39 Ardea; 38*bl* Ardea;
39*tl* NHPA; 39*tr* NHPA; 39*b* Ardea; 40 Corbis; 41 Naturepl; 41*t* Corbis; 48 Getty

Commissioned photography on pages 42–47 by Andy Crawford. Project maker and photo shoot coordinator: Miranda Kennedy
Thank you to models Anastasia Mitchell, Holly Hadaway, and Sonnie Nash.

Animal Disguises

Belinda Weber

KINGFISHER
NEW YORK

Contents

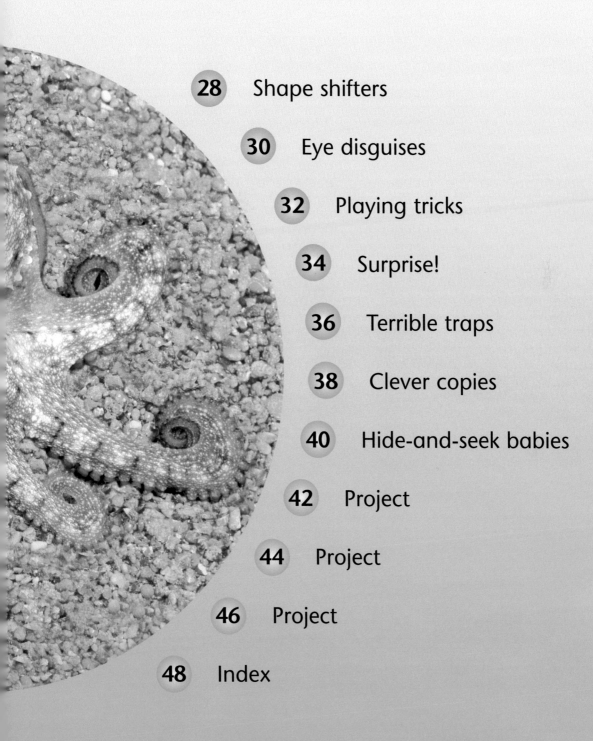

What is camouflage?

Camouflage is the way in which an animal blends in with its surroundings. It can be the animal's body shape or the color of its coat or skin that helps it match its home. Camouflage is used for two reasons—to hunt or to hide from predators.

Silent power

Creeping through the undergrowth, a tiger is difficult to see. The long grass is light colored, but its shadows look black. The light and dark lines blend in with the markings on the tiger's back.

predators—*animals that hunt and eat other animals*

Spots and stripes

Spots and stripes break up an animal's shape. At dusk or dawn, when many creatures feed, their markings blend in with the shadows, making it difficult to see each animal clearly.

Who's who?

A zebra's coat confuses predators. All the stripes merge, and it is hard to see where one zebra ends and another one begins.

Spot the leopard

During the hottest part of the day leopards like to rest in leafy trees. The leaves cast dark shadows all around. These shadows look like the spots on the leopard's coat and help camouflage it while it sleeps. The spots also help the leopard catch its food. While hunting it can move slowly through the grass, unseen by prey.

prey—an animal that is hunted and killed by other animals

Blending in

Bold colors and shapes are great disguises. In wooded areas, where there is a lot of light and shade, these bold markings make it hard to see what is a shadow and what is an animal.

Standing tall

The dark blotches on a giraffe's coat look like patches of shade. They help disguise it as it eats the acacia trees in its African habitat.

habitat—*an animal's home*

Safe in the grass

When it is first born, a baby red deer cannot run fast enough to keep up with its mother. The mother deer hides the baby in grasses where its spotty brown coat matches the light and shadows on the ground.

Super stripes

Tapirs live in rain forests. For the first six months of their lives baby tapirs have striped coats that make them hard to see in the dappled jungle light.

dappled—spots or patches of a darker color

Watch your step!

Some animals build their homes on the ground. They need to be the same color as their habitat so that predators cannot spot them. Mottled markings on their skin help them blend in.

Guard duty

Even though meerkats are the same golden color as the ground, they feel even safer when one of them is looking out for predators. Standing tall, one keeps watch while the others feed and play.

mottled—a pattern of colored patches

Living carpets

Carpet sharks look like the seabed. This is because the blotchy patches on their skin match the rocks and stones around them.

In hiding

Pheasants' feathers are multicolored, so it is hard to see them in shady light. They hide in wooded areas or in long grass.

Froggy floors

Marsupial frogs live among the fallen leaves in rain forests. Their brown, patchy skin makes them difficult to see. Even the babies look like the forest floor.

Life in a leaf

Leaves make good hiding places. Some animals hide there to catch prey by surprise. Others eat the leaves and do not want to be seen by predators.

Leafy looks

The body, legs, and head of this wandering leaf insect are shaped just like the leaves it eats.

Dead ringer

The leaf-tailed gecko scampers across the forest floor. Its body shape and color make it look like dead leaves.

tropical—an area close to the equator with very hot, dry weather

Life on the riverbed

The Suriname toad blends in perfectly with the leaves that cover the riverbed, where it lives. It hides, camouflaged, waiting for passing prey.

Lacy lichen

Lichen katydids live in tropical cloud forests. They merge almost perfectly with the lichen plants that grow there. The feathery leaves of the plant match the lacy pattern on the katydid's body.

cloud forest—a tropical mountain rain forest

Flowers and fruits

Plants often have bright flowers and tasty fruits. They need animals to help them spread their seeds. But even the prettiest flower is not always what it seems.

Pretty in pink

Lurking in this bright pink flower, a crab spider waits for a tasty meal. It holds its front legs wide apart, ready to grab its prey.

Watch out!

Hidden among the white flowers, this orchid mantis is difficult to see. If an insect flies by, the mantis will attack and eat the welcome snack.

Fruit surprise

These tasty-looking palm fruits hide a deadly secret. Waiting silently among the fruits, an eyelash viper hopes its prey will come within easy striking distance.

Stony features

A huge number of creatures live among rocks and pebbles. The different colors of the stones and the shadows they cast make great hiding places.

Stone home

An African rock python is hard to see among the stones. Its skin is mottled, so it matches the colors of the rocks perfectly. It rests on the stones while it warms up in the sun and then slides off quietly in search of prey.

Jumping stones

Stone grasshoppers have such good disguises that they are often only visible when they move. Their long back legs allow them to make powerful jumps, so they can leap away from predators.

Star spotting

The stargazer fish buries itself in the seabed to complete its disguise. The only things that give it away are its eyes and mouth, but even these look like pebbles and sand. Fish that swim too close are snapped up for a tasty meal.

visible—easy to see

Like a branch

Many animals try to look like sticks in order to fool predators. Others take on the shape of branches and hide in trees. Some predators, such as crocodiles, hope to pass as tree trunks so their prey will not notice them.

Log alike

Floating on the surface of a river, a crocodile looks just like a log. Its unlucky prey gets a terrible shock when it stops for a drink!

Walking sticks

With its long, thin body
and legs, a stick insect
is easily confused with
a twig. It even sways
gently in the wind—
just like a twig does!

Slowly, slowly

Clinging upside down
to branches, sloths creep
around their forest homes.
When it rains, algae grow
on the branches and in
the sloth's fur, helping
it hide in the trees.

algae—tiny plants

Above and **below**

Some animals have light-colored bellies and dark backs. This is a double disguise called countershading. It makes them hard to see from above and from below.

Light and dark

The lapwing has a dark gray-green back that blends in with grass. This makes it tricky to see from up in the air. But when it flies, the lapwing's white belly blends in with the light sky, so it is difficult to see from the ground.

Black and white

When it swims,
a penguin's white
belly blends in with
the lighter surface water.
From above, its dark back
looks like deep water.

Sneaky sharks

Sharks and other fish also use countershading.
A shark is able to sneak up on a school of fish
from above or below since its dark and light
coloring helps disguise its shape.

school—*a large number of fish swimming together*

New season's colors

Camouflage works only if the animal looks like its surroundings. When the weather changes, some animals have to change their coat colors so that they still look the same as their habitat.

The latest look

Snowshoe hares live in Alaska. In the summer their coats are brown in order to blend in with the ground. In the winter the hares grow new, white coats to help them stay hidden in the snow.

A new winter coat

Arctic foxes are predators
and need to be able to sneak
up on their prey. In the winter
their snowy white coats blend
in perfectly with their icy world.
In the summer their coats are
brown, so they match the
earthy colors of the season.

earthy—brown

Time to change

Chameleons are the masters of disguise. Special cells in their skin let them change their skin color to match their backgrounds. They can switch from one color to another in fewer than 15 minutes.

parson's chameleon

antsingy leaf chameleon

Colorful creatures

Chameleons are predators and
need to stay hidden until they attack
their insect prey. Whether resting
in leaves or hunting in the desert,
a chameleon can change its skin
color to match its background.

desert chameleon

***cells**—units from which all animals are made*

Shape shifters

Sometimes skin color and shape are not enough to keep an animal hidden. Sticks, stones, plants, and even clothes may be used to make a new disguise.

Living garden

Darkling beetles cover their bodies with lichen and other small plants. These plants grow and help the beetle stay hidden from predators as it searches for food.

Skillful weaver

The clothes moth larva does not like to be disturbed while it is feeding. It makes itself a coat out of whichever insect it is eating and then eats without interruption!

larva—the young stage of some animals' life cycle

Making a shell suit

A caddis fly larva's disguise is a case that grows around its body. The larva sticks shells, small pebbles, leaves, or any other small items it can find on top of this clever disguise.

Hanging decorations

A decorator crab's body is covered with tiny hooked hairs. It hangs seaweed from these hairs to help it hide on the seabed.

Eye disguises

An animal's eyes are very sensitive. If they are attacked, it can cause blindness and put the creature's life in danger. For this reason some animals have false "eyes." Others disguise their eyes with bold patterns.

Eyes down

These fruit bats rest in big groups and often squabble. To protect their eyes during fights, they have white tufts of hair beneath their ears. Attackers target these instead of the real things.

Heads or tails?

The eyes of butterfly fish are hidden in a dark stripe across their faces. They also have a false eye near the tail, so predators go for the wrong end.

sensitive—easily damaged

How many eyes?

The eyespots on this emperor
moth's wings look like eyes.
If a predator attacks them,
it is unlikely to do much harm,
and the moth can escape.

Looking back

This pearl-spotted
owlet has false eyes,
made from dark
feathers, on the
back of its head.
These decoy eyes
may confuse both
predators and
prey about
which way the
owl is looking.

decoy—designed to mislead

Playing tricks

Some animals have an extra defense when they are attacked. They behave strangely or do something unexpected that confuses the predator and stops it from attacking.

All fall down

Fainting goats perform a nifty trick when they feel threatened—they fall over in a dead faint! Once the dange has passed, the goat gets up as if nothing happened.

faint—to collapse or pass out

deflated balloon fish

Spiky mouthful

Balloon fish look like
small, tasty bites when
swimming normally, with
flattened spines. But as
soon as they are in any
danger, they gulp down
water to blow themselves
up into a big, spiky ball.
This makes them look
much less mouthwatering!

inflated balloon fish

inflated—blown up

Surprise!

Sometimes a predator holds off eating an animal if it is startled in some way. Many animals rely on surprising their attackers, and then they escape.

Which way around?

The shingleback lizard's tail looks like its head! Attackers that mistakenly go for the ta will find that the lizard races off in the other direction.

Flashing red

When resting, a fire-bellied toad looks like floating pondweed. But when startled, it rears up and flashes its red and black belly.

startled—surprised

Frilling

A frilled lizard has a flap of skin around its neck that opens up like an umbrella when it is scared.

Terrible traps

Some predators are so well disguised that prey comes too close, unaware of any risk. Others bring their prey within striking distance using a trap or lure.

Wagging tongues

The pink tip of this alligator snapping turtle's tongue wiggles like a worm. If a fish swims up to eat the worm, it becomes the turtle's dinner!

Tempting tails

The yellow end of a copperhead snake's tail looks like lunch to a frog. But if it gets too close, the frog itself ends up on the menu.

lure—an attractive-looking trap

End of the line

Anglerfish live in deep, dark oceans. They lure prey with a "fishing line" that hangs over their mouths. The end of the line glows. Fish come to look at the light and are eaten by the crafty anglers.

Clever copies

Predators learn what tastes bad or is poisonous and then avoid it. Some prey animals mimic bad-tasting animals or objects. Predators then stay away from them, too.

No sting in the tail!

Bees, wasps, and hornets have painful stings, so predators avoid them. This clearwing moth looks like a hornet, and this keeps it safe from predators.

Copy ant

Ants produce a poison to stop attackers. The mirid bug looks like an ant, and this protects it.

mimic—to copy

*Pueblan
milk snake*

*Eastern
coral snake*

Mix-up

Coral snakes are very venomous.
Milk snakes are harmless, but they
look like coral snakes. This means that
most attackers leave them both alone.

Not what it seems

Some predators are clever
mimics. This praying mantis
looks like a bird dropping!
If an insect comes close, it
soon gets snapped up.

venomous—*poisonous*

Hide-and-seek babies

Baby animals are often left alone while their parents go to find food. To keep them safe, their colorings blend in with their surroundings.

Sitting pretty

Lion cubs have sandy-colored coats that match their savanna home. They hide in the grass while their mom is away.

savanna—*stretches of dry grassland in tropical areas*

Hard to spot

Arctic tern chicks wait for their parents to bring them food. Their feathers look like the surrounding rocks, allowing them to blend in. The little chick beside the chirping one shows just how good this camouflage is.

Snow babies

Harp seal cubs live in icy places. Their white coats help them hide on the snowy ground until they are big enough to defend themselves.

Hidden homes

Make a caddis fly larva's house

Caddis fly larvae make a camouflaged case in which to live. They carry it around with them, hoping no one will notice them. You can make a disguised home for a model caddis fly larva.

You will need
- Cardboard tube
- Brown paint
- Paintbrush
- Glue
- Camouflage material: twigs, leaves, shells, stones
- Modeling clay—3 colors
- 1 yellow pipe cleaner

1

Mix some brown paint and water. Take the cardboard tube and paint it brown. Leave it to dry. This is your caddis fly larva's case.

2

Glue small twigs, dried leaves, shells, and small stones onto the cardboard tube. Make sure the tube is well covered. Leave it to dry.

3

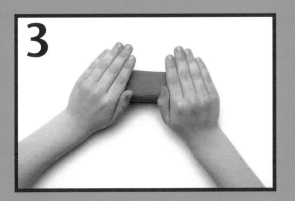

Roll some blue modeling clay into a sausage shape. Make sure it is small enough to fit inside the tube. This is the larva's body.

4

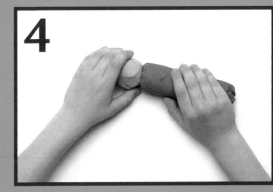

Take a smaller piece of light blue modeling clay and roll it into a ball. Attach it to the darker blue body. Your larva now has a head!

5

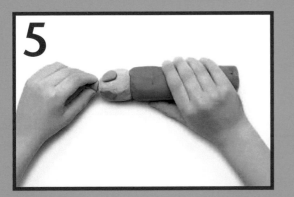

Using some green modeling clay, make two tiny flat balls for the eyes and a small cone for the mouth.

6

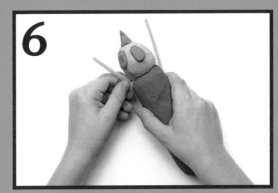

Cut a pipe cleaner in half and push each piece into opposite sides of the body. The larva is now ready to be put inside its new home.

Tiger fun

Tiger face painting

Paint your own face while looking in a mirror. Or draw tiger stripes on a friend's face and then ask him or her to paint yours.

You will need
- Face paints and brushes
- Warm water
- Soap
- Sponge

1 Start with a clean face! Put black face paint on a brush. Paint the tip of your nose and your lips. Draw a stripe under your nose.

2 With white paint, draw whiskers coming out from under your nose, across your cheeks, and around the corners of your mouth.

3 Paint black stripes under your eyes and on your forehead, chin, and cheeks. Add white stripes on your eyebrows and a dot on your nose.

4 Use red and orange paints to fill in some lines on your cheeks, chin, and forehead.

Add the finishing touches with some gold paint on your forehead, cheeks, and chin. Now that you look like a tiger it is time to test the disguise. How many people recognize you with a tiger's face?

When you have had enough of being a tiger, carefully wash off the face paints using warm water, soap, and a sponge.

Mystery picture

Draw a camouflage picture

Chameleons are masters of disguise, and these two are no exception. In this clever two-in-one picture you will need two outlines of a chameleon. To get the basic shape you can trace around the parson's chameleon on page 27.

1

Color in one of the chameleon outlines in shades of green and blue. Use oranges and purples for the second chameleon outline.

You will need

- 2 pieces of 8½ in. x 11 in. paper, each with an outline of a chameleon on it
- Scissors
- A piece of paper that measures at least 11 in. x 17 in.
- Colored markers
- Ruler
- Pencil
- Glue

2

Finish adding backgrounds to both pictures. Using a ruler and a pencil, draw lines down both pictures that are around one inch apart.

3

Carefully cut along the lines so that your pictures are in long, thin strips. Stack them in order, with the chameleon head on top.

4 Take the long piece of paper. Glue the top strip of the green picture on the left. Next to it paste the first strip of the purple picture. Continue doing this until there are no strips left. When the paper is dry, fold the new picture along the edges of the strips into a zigzag shape.

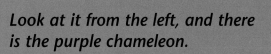

Look at the picture from the right, and you will see the green chameleon.

Look at it from the left, and there is the purple chameleon.

Index